MUSH!

BY JOE FUNK

Sled Dogs
OF THE Iditarod

SCHOLASTIC INC.

ISBN 978-0-545-49478-6

12 11 10 9 8 7 6 5 4 3 2 1   13 14 15 16 17 18/0

Printed in the U.S.A.   40

First edition, January 2013

Created and designed by Mojo Media Inc.: Author/Editor, Joe Funk; Assistant Editor, Rob Jaskula; Art Director, Daniel Tideman

When Dallas Seavey stood atop the podium in 2012 in Nome, Alaska with two of his favorite dogs, lead dogs Diesel and Guiness, he broke into a wide smile. He comes from a huge family of successful mushers and is considered one of the best athletes in the sport. A former state and national champion wrestler, he is often considered the best athlete in any competition he is in.

His grandfather Dan Seavey competed in the first two Iditarods. He led for just about half of the first

MEET THE RACE CHAMPS

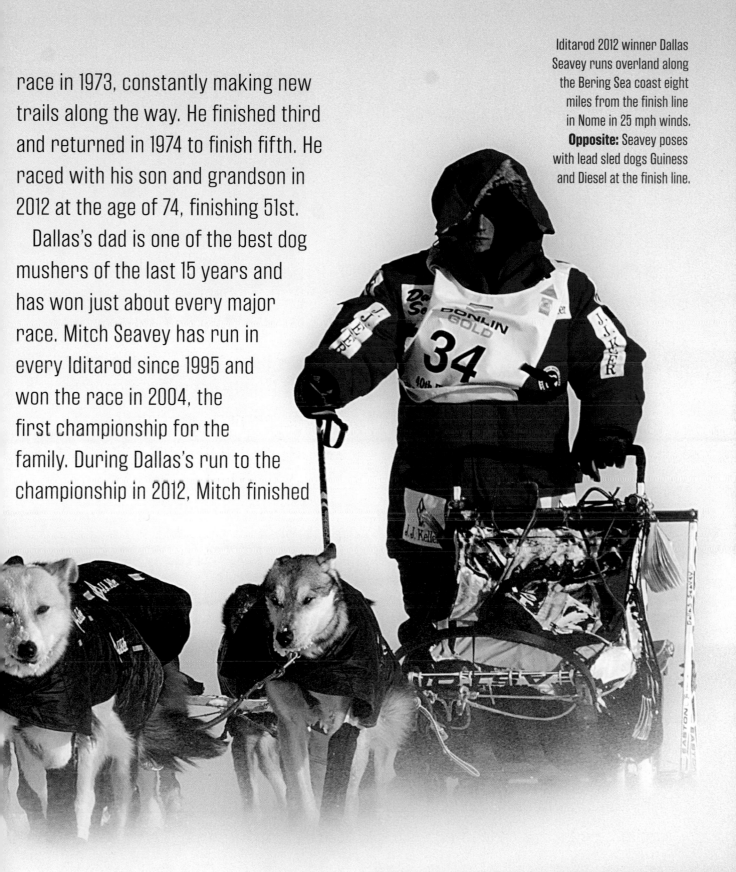

race in 1973, constantly making new trails along the way. He finished third and returned in 1974 to finish fifth. He raced with his son and grandson in 2012 at the age of 74, finishing 51st.

Dallas's dad is one of the best dog mushers of the last 15 years and has won just about every major race. Mitch Seavey has run in every Iditarod since 1995 and won the race in 2004, the first championship for the family. During Dallas's run to the championship in 2012, Mitch finished

Iditarod 2012 winner Dallas Seavey runs overland along the Bering Sea coast eight miles from the finish line in Nome in 25 mph winds. **Opposite:** Seavey poses with lead sled dogs Guiness and Diesel at the finish line.

seventh. Two of Dallas's brothers, Danny and Tyrell, also have raced in the Iditarod.

At the age of 25, Dallas is the youngest man ever to win the Iditarod. In 2005, he was the youngest person to ever finish the race. He slowly became a top-level competitor and took time out to marry his wife, Jen, who he raced against in the 2009 Iditarod.

In 2011, it had become clear that Dallas was going to be a successful musher like his dad. In his fifth Iditarod, he finished fourth. It was his best finish of his career and marked the third straight year that he had finished in the top 10.

He had warmed up for that Iditarod by running a different 1,000 mile race, the Yukon Quest. Run before the Iditarod, it takes place in the winter and goes from Fairbanks, Alaska, to Whitehorse, Yukon, in Canada. Though the Iditarod is the more famous race,

Michelle Phillips on the Chena River at the start of the 2006 Yukon Quest sled dog race.

Circle City

YUKON

Fairbanks

Dawson City

Stewart River

Carmacks

Braeburn

ALASKA

Whitehorse

YUKON QUEST DOG SLED RACE ROUTE

the Yukon Quest is just as hard. Many Iditarod champions have won both races, but only one race rookie had won the Yukon Quest before Dallas accomplished the feat in 2011.

To win, he came up with a strategy that he still uses — sitting back early before attacking late. This was important in the Yukon Quest since the weather was worse than usual and nearly half the teams were forced out of the race.

A musher is only as good as his dogs. Dallas is well known for his love of his dogs. Seavey was building a

Guiness was awarded the City of Nome Lolly Medley Golden Harness Award, given to the best canine athlete at the Iditarod.

Dallas Seavey's dogs sleep in the warm sun at the Shageluk village checkpoint during the 2011 Iditarod race.

MUSH!

great team in 2011 and said that he had a chance to win the Iditarod in 2012. Mostly made up of younger dogs, except for nine-year-old Guiness, his 2012 Iditarod team was fast and powerful.

Guiness had been Seavey's lead dog for several years, but as her career was nearing its end, Seavey turned to Diesel more often to lead. Still, Guiness and three other dogs also spent time in the lead role in the Iditarod.

Guiness has been with Seavey for most of his mushing career. She is a tough dog who keeps her teammates in line, helping with the younger dogs so Dallas doesn't have to worry about them. She is a black-and-tan-colored husky.

She had some of her finest moments in the 2012 Iditarod. Since Seavey uses so many dogs in the lead role, each one has their strengths. For Guiness, it's the tough sections that require brains and an attitude. She works best when the trail is hard, saving the team hours each time she faces a challenge. She's not very big, weighing just 40 pounds.

Dallas likes working her in the lead role in those difficult sections. Since they know each other so well and he can trust her, Guiness is allowed to run at a faster pace. Because sled dogs have such amazing memories of the trail, Guiness's experience is very important to the team. Guiness usually runs with Roadie, a bigger, light-colored husky who likes to chew on the harness lines.

Diesel is the rising star of Seavey's team. Five years old and the biggest dog in the pack, he has worked in just about every role on the team. Strong and a natural athlete, Dallas thinks that Diesel has the ability to be the best sled dog in the world.

Careful training built him up to the point where he could take the lead role, and he has been a star ever since, making the hardest runs look easy.

Derby is one of Seavey's most beloved dogs, a tough husky who once lost half of his tail in a fight. He is a very happy boy but likes to start fights, even though he almost

Dallas Seavey on the Yukon River shortly after leaving the Ruby checkpoint, Iditarod 2012.

Dog mushing is such a family affair for the Seaveys that they have made a tourism business out of it. They operate Ididaride Sled Dog Tours to teach the public about Iditarod-style sled dog racing, which also serves as a chance to train their racing dogs. Dallas and his wife, Jen, run another business in Anchorage: WildRide Sled Dog Rodeo.

always loses. He is tough to handle sometimes but loves his life as a racing sled dog and is always happy to be in the middle of a race.

Though only Diesel and Guiness got to go up on the podium with Dallas and wear flower wreaths, all nine of the dogs he finished the Iditarod with are stars in their own way.

There is another Seavey younger than Dallas that hopes to run the Iditarod in 2015. Conway Seavey, who is also a musician, has been training to mush dogs since he could walk. He has won a number of junior races and might be the next famous Seavey.

First-place finisher Dallas Seavey runs down the finish chute in Nome, Iditarod 2012. **Inset:** Dallas Seavey poses with his lead dogs Diesel and Guiness at the musher's finisher banquet in Nome after Iditarod 2012.

Dallas Seavey mushes through a ski trail lined with spectators in midtown Anchorage, Alaska, during the 2012 Iditarod ceremonial start.

THE WINNING ROUTE

It was a perfect day to race sleds as the ceremonial start from Anchorage to Campbell Airstrip kicked off the 2012 Iditarod. With the race following its northern route, the 975 miles ahead were going to be tough, cold, and lonely for the mushers and their dogs. Dallas Seavey was not a favorite as he started his sixth Iditarod, as there were several repeat champions in the field.

The ceremonial start allowed everyone to get their feet wet before the racers were moved to the town of Willow.

There, the racers start again, in the same order as Anchorage, which is decided in a pre-race drawing. Dallas Seavey was in the middle of the field, one place ahead of his dad. The race finally set off from Willow, and it was action-packed from the start.

Since there are certain rests that mushers have to take, it is important to know how hard to push the dogs before taking the breaks. Dallas's plan was to sit back and let other teams tire out racing toward the checkpoints, taking breaks often. He was going to wait until near the end of the race to make his move.

It was cold outside, but there was no snow in the air and things were going smoothly. Two former champions led the way into Finger Lake: John Baker had set the race's speed record the year before, and Lance Mackey had won the race four times in a row before that.

Dallas was sitting back, thinking

that the tight racing at the front would cause all of the former champions to fade as the race continued and their dogs tired. Baker and Mackey were passed going to Rainy Pass, the highest point on the Iditarod trail at over 3,000 feet. Dallas stayed back in the pack, still waiting to make his move.

All 66 racers, including the three Seavey teams, made it to the checkpoint at Nikolai. Mitch was leading the family in sixth, with Dallas in tenth, and Dan bringing up the rear in last place.

Aliy Zirkle led the race into the checkpoint before leaving for McGrath, a town of 400 people 48 miles away. The next checkpoint was Takotna, a popular spot to take the 24-hour rest. Though the leaders stopped there, some of the racers elected to skip the stop, such as father and son Martin and Rohn Buser, who took the lead — at least until they stopped for their 24-hour break.

Eating on the trail is tough. If mushers take their 24-hour layover in Takotna, they can order fresh cheeseburgers and eat as many homemade pies as they want.

Mitch Seavey passes under the Kouwegok Slough bridge shortly after leaving Unalakleet at midday, Iditarod 2012.

Lance Mackey drops onto Long Lake at the restart of Iditarod 2012 in Willow, Alaska.

Rohn Buser's team heads down the trail after leaving the Ophir checkpoint, Iditarod 2012.

Kouwegok Slough

Dallas's strategy was beginning to pay off. By not racing to the front in the early stages, his dogs were ready to run. Diesel was taking the lead most of the time and the team was moving well.

The route was about to get very difficult. After Ophir, the teams had to run 73 miles to Cripple, the halfway point of the race. The first musher to get there wins $3,000, paid in gold nuggets. From there it was another 70 miles to the next checkpoint, in Ruby.

Jim Lanier, a 71-year-old musher, had not taken his 24-hour break yet and was the first to Cripple. He had slept just three hours in four days, and claimed the gold nuggets.

Ruby is the first checkpoint of the difficult Yukon River stretch of the race, and Mitch Seavey was the first to arrive. He and Dallas decided to take their second required break, this time just eight hours, while they were there. Aliy Zirkle decided to press on, running her dogs hard to try and put some space in between her and the Seaveys.

It was 10 degrees below zero as Dallas left Ruby with 14 dogs on his sled, two fewer than he started with. Dogs are frequently taken off of their sleds due to exhaustion or veterinarian recommendation to preserve their health. Dallas eventually had to remove seven dogs by the end of the race.

The stretch to the next checkpoint in Galena was going to be tough, since it was very cold outside, with the temperature expected to dip to 20 degrees below zero during the day. Dallas put Guiness in the lead for this part of the race, counting on his reliable veteran dog to get through the toughest parts of the race.

With their rests done, the top mushers raced on, heading through Galena. Only three hours separated

Veterinarian Elizabeth King examining Aaron Burmeister's dogs at the Finger Lake checkpoint during Iditarod 2012. **Left**: Burmeister's dog Inuk rests during an eight-hour layover at White Mountain checkpoint.

Takotna is a popular place for the 24-hour rest that all teams must take. There is a building there with a 24-hour kitchen and a full staff, who are known for making excellent pies. Dallas, along with many of the other race leaders, decided to take their day-long rest there.

Jeff King on the Yukon River shortly after leaving the village of Ruby, Alaska, Iditarod 2012.

the top teams, and it was clear that two men had the fastest teams: Dallas Seavey and Aaron Burmeister.

The teams rolled into Kaltag nearly even. Burmeister made it in and out of the checkpoint in Unalakleet first. Just 220 miles from the finish, he could not hold the lead. Dallas Seavey decided it was time to attack as he passed Burmeister.

The extra rest was about to really pay off for Dallas — the next stretch of the trail went 170 miles through several checkpoints, with an eight-hour break waiting at White Mountain. Since his dogs were well rested, Dallas could push his team to the checkpoint. It was believed that the first musher to arrive there would win the race.

He built his lead up to as much as three hours at the checkpoint in Elim on the way to White Mountain, racing through the checkpoints. He continued to rest his dogs in short bursts, though Aliy Zirkle raced hard and at one point got within a mile of Dallas.

Dallas was first to White Mountain thanks to one more advantage he had. Since he is such a good athlete,

Dallas Seavey shakes hands with the crowd in the chute as he wins the 2012 Iditarod, Nome, Alaska.

Dallas can run behind his sled for a long time during races without falling behind. This is easier on the dogs, and in the race to White Mountain, it allowed him to get there more than an hour before Zirkle.

It was clear now that the man who turned 25 on the first real day of the race was going to win the Iditarod. There were just 77 miles left to Nome, and no one was going to catch him.

With nine dogs on his sled, Dallas turned down Front Street in Nome an hour ahead of Zirkle to claim the 40th Iditarod, making history as the youngest person to win the race. 🐾

Aliy Zirkle arrives first to the McGrath checkpoint in the Iditarod 2012 and wins the PenAir Spirit of Alaska Award.

BALTO & THE SLED BREED

Dogs — man's best friend — have been loyal workers and pets ever since the first gray wolves were tamed. Domesticating the animals took a long time, but dogs have been at their human masters' sides for well over 10,000 years.

Though now seen mainly as house pets, most dog breeds have a history as a worker of some type. Using selective breeding, people were able to create different types of dogs suited for different tasks. From hunting to herding, pulling loads, chasing rats, or keeping people safe, dogs are great at many jobs.

All breeds are part of the same species and can trace their roots to wild gray wolves. They were gradually tamed by humans until they were accustomed to living with people. As humans migrated around the world and used dogs for many purposes, they bred dogs suited for living in different climates or for doing certain jobs,

Today's huskies are bred to be bigger than their Siberian counterpart. The Alaskan husky is not yet a distinct breed of dog, but they are a bit different than their ancestors.

Eight-week-old Iditarod husky pups sit in an antique wooden sled in Nome during the 2010 Iditarod.

Alaskan malamute

leading to the first distinct dog breeds.

The husky is considered an ancient dog, tracing its roots back thousands of years to Siberia, which is a part of Russia.

Known for being one of the coldest places on earth, Siberia is a tough place to live. To survive, people must make the most of what they have and live simply, since there is not much margin for error in such a harsh environment. Bred to be a hauling dog, huskies were born to pull sleds in cold climates. This is why they are by far the best sled dogs — it's what they were made to do!

The temperatures in Siberia can reach 100 degrees below zero, and winds can blow as strong as

Though many racing dogs today are crossbreeds, the husky is by far the most popular purebred. Alaskan malamutes are about twice the size of huskies but are slower.

Robert Peary, a man who claimed to be the first to reach the North Pole, did so in 1909 with a team of huskies hauling his gear.

Robert Peary in 1908.

hurricanes, so the dogs needed to not just survive but thrive in the frigid cold. Dogs gave humans the ability to travel up to 100 miles to fishing sites around Siberia, making it easier to reach their food supply.

As such, huskies were very important to the people of Siberia. The best dogs were owned by the richest and most powerful people. Women raised the puppies while men trained the dogs for their work on the sleds. Children got to enjoy their company and warmth at night.

Every year, the Siberian tribes met to trade. In the early 1900s, explorers were starting to make contact with them, as there was a push in the Western world to explore the polar regions and reach the poles.

In 1908, a Russian fur trader named William Goosak brought a team of the dogs across the Bering Sea, introducing them to Alaska for the first time.

After he arrived, Goosak decided to race in the 1909 All Alaska Sweepstakes, a 408-mile sled race. The Alaskan gold rush had made sled-pulling dogs an important part of life as Alaska began to expand, and the races were a form of entertainment.

Huskies and dogs like them are part of a group called Spitz dogs. They are known for being able to live in the cold and for being hearty, tough animals.

When the huskies showed up — much smaller than the other dogs — they were laughed at by the locals. About half the weight of the common malamute and much smaller in height, the "Siberian wolf dogs" were given little chance. But the huskies eventually finished third after leading for much of the race.

One man named Fox Maule Ramsay was inspired after seeing how strong the little dogs ran and spent $25,000 to bring 70 dogs from Siberia for the race. Split into three different teams, the huskies took first, second, and fourth places. The husky was about to change Alaska.

By 1914, though, only about 15 of the original dogs remained. A man from Norway named Leonhard Seppala bought the remaining dogs and entered the All Alaska Sweepstakes. "The little man with his little dogs" dominated the race and became famous throughout Alaska.

Huskies gained international recognition in 1925. An outbreak of diphtheria in isolated Nome set off a panic, and the only medicine that could save the sick people was in Anchorage, 1,000 miles away. There was an airplane nearby, but it wouldn't start. The medicine had to travel by dog.

Seppala and his dogs, led by Togo, were a part of a 20-musher team that brought the medicine to Nome. The last leg was driven by another Norwegian, Gunnar Kaasen, and his lead dog, Balto.

Balto knew the route and was able to lead a run through conditions that might have stopped other teams. Running mostly in darkness, Balto led the sled into Nome with the medicine and helped save the town.

Balto became a celebrity and traveled throughout the United States. To this day, a statue of him stands in Central Park in New York City. The husky is now recognized around the world, and what the Siberians knew for thousands of years is no longer a secret — the husky is one amazing dog. ❖

Leonhard Seppalla

Gunnar Kaasen and Balto

Early mushers faced difficult conditions and used equipment
far different and less advanced than today.

TOOLS 🐾
& TRAILS

Most early equipment was made from natural materials such as wood and animal hides.

Hundreds of years before people from Russia arrived in Alaska, natives used parts of the modern Iditarod trail to move around the wilderness. This native route became a popular "highway" for settlers, as dogsleds became the only possible form of transportation for people, goods, and supplies during the harsh and long Alaskan winters.

The long winters closed down many mining towns, so races between dogsled teams became very popular.

Big events like the All Alaska Sweepstakes captured the attention of many people just after the 1900s began, as teams from all over the territory began to compete. Since the races were getting serious, better dogs and gear were needed.

The original sleds were heavy and made out of sturdy wood, so it took a lot of effort for the dogs to pull them. New racing sleds were built for the competitions, designed to be lighter and turn easier.

The more modern wood sleds featured steel or iron runners on the bottom of the sled, able to glide along the surface like an ice skate. Dogs were mainly fed meat that was hunted along the way, since dog food as we know it didn't exist yet. Today, they get very healthy food, and get

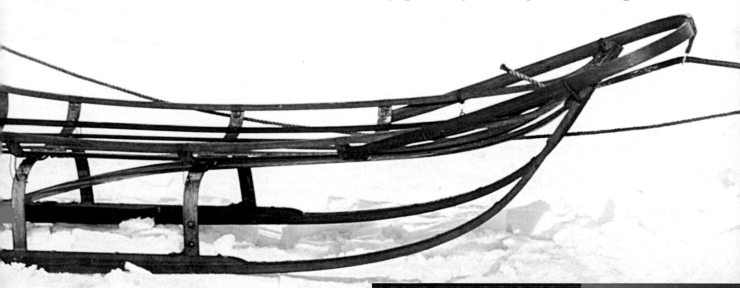

top training and medical care, since they are professional athletes.

The new wooden sleds were still too heavy, so as the years went on, newer materials were used. Plastic and carbon fiber materials came into use in the second half of the 20th century, making sleds lighter than ever.

The last 30 years have seen even more rapid changes. Booties for the dogs' feet used to be socks made for children and tied on with tape. Today, they're made of a nylon created specifically for the dogs and held together with Velcro so they can last all day without needing to be changed. Dogs with sensitive feet that might not have been able to race in the past can now compete, thanks to the booties.

The breeding of the dogs is the most important advancement in how the Iditarod is raced. Endurance and speed are the two most important things needed in a sled dog, and Siberian huskies quickly proved to be the best.

Dog harnesses were originally made of animal hides but are now fabricated using materials such as nylon, and attach to the dogs from many different ways and angles. Depending on the pulling position of the dogs in the team, they each wear a custom harness designed to maximize their pulling power.

During her 24-hour layover, Karin Hendrickson takes each dog for a walk and playtime at the Takotna checkpoint. Here she plays with Cutter, Iditarod 2012.

John Suter holding two of the poodles from his dog team during the 1988 Iditarod.

Ray Redington, Jr., feeds his dogs shortly after arriving at the Nikolai checkpoint.

Today, huskies are bred with other dogs to make bigger, faster racing dogs: the Alaskan husky. Though not a breed of its own, good mixes of this type are the elite of the sport.

Other breeds of dogs have raced in the Iditarod; between 1988 and 1991, one team that raced was made up entirely of standard poodles.

The way the race is run has also changed. The Iditarod is a little bit shorter than it once was, covering 975 miles in 2012, after being more than 1,100 miles in years past. Mushers used to rest their dogs for longer than they ran, but now dogs race for longer by running a bit slower.

Mushers have to eat, but there are not many choices on the trail. They used to cut down trees to build fires for cooking and warmth, but since this took a long time they began to carry small gas stoves with them. These were heavy and hard to use, so now alcohol cookers are used for cooking, heating, and to melt snow to turn into water for the dogs.

Sleds have gotten more comfortable,

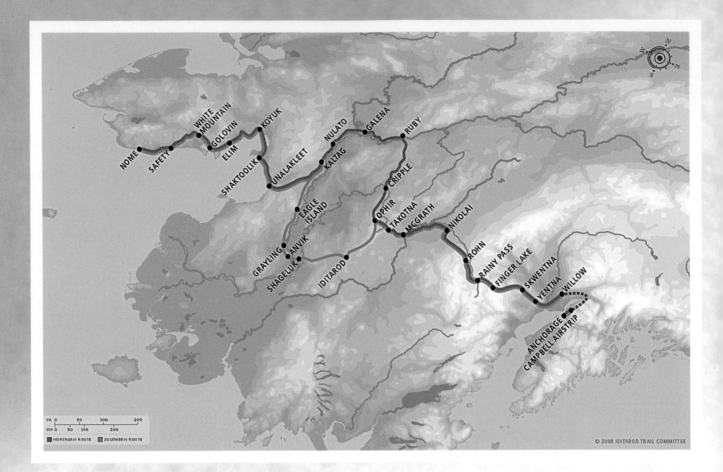

too, thanks to mushers like Jeff King. King is well known among mushers for always finding new ways to make life easier on the trail. His sled with a seat on the back is the most comfortable way to race, and the heated handgrips he invented keep mushers warm and can be used to melt snow into water for thirsty dogs.

Today's Iditarod uses two routes, changed each year. Both versions start in Anchorage for the ceremonial start and then go to Ophir, where the race route turns to the north in even-numbered years and to the south in odd-numbered years. Both routes meet back up in Kaltag, 441 miles from the finish in Nome.

Even the prizes are unique: The first musher to cross Cripple Creek wins a pile of gold nuggets, while the final team to cross the finish line is awarded the Red Lantern trophy.

Modern racers send most of their

gear by plane from Anchorage to various checkpoints along the way. They send food, booties, runners and sometimes even entire sleds ahead to use later in the race.

Mushers are more comfortable now than ever, thanks to new fabrics used in making winter clothes. The lighter their clothing, the easier it is for them to move and the more comfortable they will be. Sleeping bags are now warmer than ever — important since staying warm at night is one of the biggest concerns for mushers. New blankets also help the dogs to stay warm when they are resting and huddled together.

Overall, the Iditarod has seen many changes in its history, but the core purpose of the race will never change. Over 1,000 miles of the hardest conditions on earth, a musher and a team of dogs race against 60 other teams to claim the Iditarod title in the last true, great outdoor race. 🐾

HALL OF FAME

DYNAMIC DOGS & THEIR LOYAL HANDLERS

Larry

A winner in seven different 1,000 mile races who has won three Golden Harness awards — twice in the Yukon Quest and once in the Iditarod — Larry is the most successful racing dog ever.

Larry continued to race for other competitors after Mackey thought about retiring him. The strong, serious dog found a second career as the lead dog for Jamaican musher Newton Marshall. Larry enjoys a worldwide following on Facebook, and patches bearing his image appear on jackets all over Alaska.

2007 Iditarod champion Lance Mackey and his lead dog Larry pose at the Nome awards banquet.

Velvet & Snickers

The lead dogs that enabled John Baker to set the Iditarod speed record in 2011, Velvet and Snickers, are fast, dependable dogs who won the Golden Harness for their performance.

The pair usually spends the entirety of every race at the front together. They are reliable, predictable dogs that love working together. Baker is the envy of other mushers for how well behaved his lead dogs are.

IDITAROD

CHAMPION
2011

 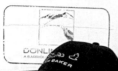 Anchorage
Chrysler Dodge
Jeep

ExxonMobil

53

IDITAROD '11
www.iditarod.com

Salem

The dog that saved Jeff King's 2006 Iditarod, Salem is an obedient dog who had the full trust of King as well as the other dogs on his team. With King shooting for a fourth Iditarod title in 2006 at the age of 50, he counted on Salem for a victory.

Salem was the hero when one of King's wheel dogs broke free from her harness and ran off. King stopped the sled and went after the runaway, but when he called her name the other dogs began running, thinking King was talking to them. With his dogs and sled moving out of sight and 35-mile-per-hour winds blowing, King yelled out to Salem to stop. When he came over a hill carrying the runaway in his arms, King saw Salem and his other dogs calmly sitting on the trail waiting for their musher.

Kuling

When Jessie Royer's lead dog Kuling won the Golden Harness in 2009, it may have come as a surprise to some. Kuling had just finished her seventh straight Iditarod, but her musher had only finished in eighth place. The real story is that Kuling is one of the most amazing racing dogs in competition today.

Kuling — whose name means "strong wind" in Swedish — is the master of the sprint across Norton Bay. Kuling raced through strong headwinds while running alone in the lead for Royer, covering the distance faster than any other team by an hour and moving them from tenth to fourth place. Kuling was recognized as one of the best dogs on the trail during her career, which ended in 2011.

MUSH! TRIVIA

IDITAROD TRAIL HEADQUARTERS

Who were the two family members that Dallas Seavey raced against in the 2012 Iditarod?

ANSWER:
HIS DAD, MITCH, AND HIS GRANDFATHER DAN

The final person to finish the Iditarod every year wins what prize?

ANSWER:
THE RED LANTERN

Dallas took two of his lead dogs to the podium after he won the Iditarod; who were they?

ANSWER:
GUINESS AND DIESEL

What race from the early 1900s was the elite sled-dog race?

ANSWER:
THE ALL ALASKA SWEEPSTAKES

One star musher is well known among his peers for his skill as an inventor, coming up with new equipment to make life on the trail easier. **Who is he?**

ANSWER:
JEFF KING. HIS INVENTIONS INCLUDE SEATS FOR THE BACK OF SLEDS AND HEATED HANDGRIPS.

What were huskies called when they first came to Alaska?

ANSWER:
SIBERIAN WOLF DOGS

The first musher to arrive in Cripple every year wins a prize; what is it?

ANSWER:
$3,000 WORTH OF GOLD NUGGETS

The Last Great Race" 1049 miles ANCHORAGE TO NOME
IDITAROD TRAIL
RACE 12

GCI   DONLIN GOLD   ANCHORAGE CHRYSLER·DODGE·JEEP·RAM   ExxonMobil

Fred Meyer   HORIZON LINES   Alaska Airlines

START

Eagle Pack

Kirk Barnum leaves the restart of Iditarod 2012 in Willow, Alaska.